God Will Use
This for Good

God Will Use This for Good

SURVIVING THE MESS OF LIFE

MAX LUCADO

THOMAS NELSON
Since 1798

NASHVILLE   DALLAS   MEXICO CITY   RIO DE JANEIRO

Published in Nashville, Tennessee, by Thomas Nelson. Thomas Nelson is a registered trademark of Thomas Nelson, Inc.

Thomas Nelson, Inc. titles may be purchased in bulk for educational, business, fund-raising, or sales promotional use. For information, please e-mail SpecialMarkets@ThomasNelson.com.

Unless otherwise noted, Scripture quotations are taken from the New King James Version®. © 1982 by Thomas Nelson, Inc. Used by permission. All rights reserved.

Other Scripture references are from the following sources: *The Message* (MSG) by Eugene H. Peterson. © 1993, 1994, 1995, 1996, 2000, 2001, 2002. Used by permission of NavPress Publishing Group. All rights reserved. New American Standard Bible® (NASB). © The Lockman Foundation 1960, 1962, 1963, 1968, 1971, 1972, 1973, 1975, 1977, 1995. Used by permission. Holy Bible, New International Version®, NIV® (NIV). © 1973, 1978, 1984 by Biblica, Inc.™ Used by permission of Zondervan. All rights reserved worldwide. www.zondervan.com

Library of Congress Cataloging-in-Publication Data is available

ISBN: 978-0-8499-2240-4
978-0-8499-4754-4 (shrink wrapped)
978-0-8499-2239-8 (with self-shipper)

Printed in the United States of America

15 16 17 RRD 6 5 4

Contents

v

A Prayer in the Dark Times

Dear Jesus,

It's a good thing you were born at night. This world sure seems dark. I have a good eye for silver linings. But they seem dimmer lately.

The whole world seems on edge. Trigger-happy. Ticked off. We hear threats of chemical weapons and nuclear

———

bombs. Are we one button-push away from annihilation?

Your world seems a bit darker these days. But you were born in the dark, right? You came at night. The shepherds were nightshift workers. The wise men followed a star. Your first cries were heard in the shadows. To see your face Mary and Joseph needed a candle flame. It was dark. Dark with Herod's jealousy. Dark with Roman oppression. Dark with poverty. Dark with violence.

Herod went on a rampage, killing babies. Joseph took you and your mom into Egypt. You were an immigrant before you were a Nazarene.

Oh, Lord Jesus, you entered the dark world of your day. Won't you enter ours? We are weary of bloodshed and pain. We, like the wise men, are looking for a

———

star. We, like the shepherds, are kneeling at a manger.

We ask you, heal us, help us, be born anew in us.

Hopefully,
Your Children

CHAPTER 1

An Audacious Promise

She had a tremble to her, the inner tremble you could feel with just a hand on her shoulder. I saw her in a grocery store. Had not seen her in some months. I asked about her kids and husband, and when I did, her eyes watered, her chin quivered, and the story spilled out. He'd left her. After twenty years of marriage, three kids, and a dozen moves, gone. Traded her in for a younger model. She did her best to maintain her composure but couldn't. The grocery store produce section became a sanctuary of sorts. Right there between the tomatoes and the heads of lettuce, she wept. We prayed. Then I said, "You'll get through this. It won't be painless. It won't be quick. But God will use this mess for good. In the meantime don't be foolish or naive. But don't despair either. With God's help you will get through this."

Two days later a friend called. He'd just been fired. The dismissal was his fault. He'd made stupid, inappropriate remarks at work. Crude, offensive statements. His boss kicked him out. Now he's a fifty-seven-year-old unemployed manager in a rotten economy. He feels terrible and sounds worse. Wife angry. Kids confused. He needed assurance, so I gave it: "You'll get through this. It won't be painless. It won't be quick. But God will use this mess for good. In the meantime don't be foolish or naive. But don't despair either. With God's help you will get through this."

Then there is the teenager I met at the café where she works. She's fresh out of high school, hoping to get into college next month. Her life, as it turns out, hasn't been easy. When she was six years old, her parents divorced. When she was fifteen, they remarried, only to divorce again a few months ago. Recently her parents told her to choose:

———

live with Mom or live with Dad. She got misty-eyed as she described their announcement. I didn't have a chance to tell her this, but if I see her again, you can bet your sweet September I am going to look her square in the eyes and say, "You'll get through this. It won't be painless. It won't be quick. But God will use this mess for good. In the meantime don't be foolish or naive. But don't despair either. With God's help you will get through this."

Audacious of me, right? How dare I say such words? Where did I get the nerve to speak such a promise into tragedy? In a pit, actually. A deep, dark pit. So steep the boy could not climb out. Had he been able to, his brothers would have shoved him back down. They were the ones who had thrown him in.

———

So it came to pass, when Joseph
had come to his brothers, that they
stripped Joseph of his tunic, the
tunic of many colors that was on
him. Then they took him and cast
him into a pit. And the pit was
empty; there was no water in it.

And they sat down to eat a meal.
(Gen. 37:23–25)

It was an abandoned cistern. Jagged
rocks and roots extended from its sides.
The seventeen-year-old boy lay at the
bottom. Downy beard, spindly arms
and legs. His hands were bound, ankles
tied. He lay on his side, knees to chest,
cramped in the small space. The sand
was wet with spittle, where he had
drooled. His eyes were wide with fear.
His voice was hoarse from screaming. It

---

wasn't that his brothers didn't hear him. Twenty-two years later, when a famine had tamed their swagger and guilt had dampened their pride, they would confess, "We saw the anguish of his soul when he pleaded with us, and we would not hear" (42:21).

These are the great-grandsons of Abraham. The sons of Jacob. Couriers of God's covenant to a galaxy of people. Tribes will bear their banners. The name of Jesus Christ will appear on their family tree. They are the Scriptures' equivalent of royalty. Yet on this day they were the Bronze Age version of a dysfunctional family.

They could have had their own reality TV show. In the shadow of a sycamore, in earshot of Joseph's appeals, they chewed on venison and passed the wineskin. Cruel and oafish. Hearts as hard as the Canaanite desert. Lunch mattered more than their brother. They despised the boy. "They hated him and could not speak peaceably to him . . . they hated him even more . . . they hated him . . . his brothers envied him" (37:4–5, 8, 11).

Here's why. Their father pampered Joseph like a prized calf. Jacob had two wives, Leah and Rachel, but one love, Rachel. When Rachel died, Jacob kept her memory alive by fawning over their first son. The brothers worked all day. Joseph played all day. They wore clothes from a secondhand store. Jacob gave Joseph a hand-stitched, multicolored cloak with embroidered sleeves. They slept in the bunkhouse. He had a queen-sized bed in his own room. While they ran the family herd, Joseph, Daddy's little darling, stayed home. Jacob treated the eleventh-born like a firstborn. The brothers spat at the sight of Joseph.

To say the family was in crisis would be like saying a grass hut might be unstable in a hurricane.

The brothers caught Joseph far from home, sixty miles away from Daddy's protection, and went nuclear on him. "They *stripped* Joseph of his tunic . . . they *took* him and *cast* him into a pit" (vv. 23–24).[1] Defiant verbs. They wanted not only to kill Joseph but also hide his body. This was a murderous cover-up from the get-go. "We shall say, 'Some wild beast has devoured him'" (v. 20).

Joseph didn't see this assault coming. He didn't climb out of bed that morning and think, *I'd better dress in padded clothing because this is the day I get tossed into a hole.* The attack caught him off guard.

So did yours. Joseph's pit came in the form of a cistern. Maybe yours came in the form of a diagnosis, a foster home, or a traumatic injury. Joseph was thrown in a hole and despised. And you? Thrown in an unemployment line and forgotten. Thrown into a divorce and abandoned, into a bed and abused. The pit. A kind of death, waterless and austere. Some people never recover. Life is reduced to one quest: get out and never be hurt again. Not simply done. Pits have no easy exits.

Joseph's story got worse before it got better. Abandonment led to enslavement, then entrapment, and finally imprisonment. He was sucker punched.

Sold out. Mistreated. People made promises only to break them, offered gifts only to take them back. If hurt were a swampland, then Joseph was sentenced to a life of hard labor in the Everglades.

Yet he never gave up. Bitterness never staked its claim. Anger never metastasized into hatred. His heart never hardened; his resolve never vanished. He not only survived; he thrived. He ascended like a helium balloon. An Egyptian official promoted him to chief servant. The prison warden placed him over the inmates. And Pharaoh, the highest ruler on the planet, shoulder-tapped Joseph to serve as his prime minister. By the end of his life, Joseph was the second most powerful man of his generation. It is not hyperbole to state

that he saved the world from starvation.
How would that look on a résumé?

Joseph
Son of Jacob
Graduate with honors from the University of
Hard Knocks
Director of Global Effort to Save Humanity
Succeeded

How? How did he flourish in the
midst of tragedy? We don't have to
speculate. Some twenty years later the
roles were reversed, Joseph as the strong
one and his brothers the weak ones.
They came to him in dread. They feared
he would settle the score and throw them
into a pit of his own making. But Joseph
didn't. And in his explanation we find
his inspiration.

———

As for you, you meant evil against me, but God meant it for good in order to bring about this present result, to preserve many people alive. (Genesis 50:20 NASB)

CHAPTER 2

Eventual Good

I n God's hands intended evil becomes eventual good. That's the message of Genesis 50:20 and the heart of Joseph's story. He tied himself to the pillar of this promise and held on for dear life. Nothing in his story glosses over the *presence* of evil. Quite the contrary. Bloodstains, tearstains are everywhere. Joseph's heart was rubbed raw against the rocks of disloyalty and miscarried justice. Yet time and time again God redeemed the pain. The torn robe became a royal one. The pit became a palace. The broken family grew old together. The very acts intended to destroy God's servant turned out to strengthen him.

"You *meant* evil against me," Joseph told his brothers, using a Hebrew verb that traces its meaning to "weave" or "plait."[1] "You *wove* evil," he was saying, "but God *rewove* it together for good."

God, the Master Weaver. He stretches the yarn and intertwines the colors, the ragged twine with the velvet strings, the pains with the pleasures. Nothing escapes his reach. Every king, despot, weather pattern, and molecule are at his command. He passes the shuttle back and forth across the generations, and as he does, a design emerges. Satan weaves; God reweaves.

And God, the Master Builder. This is the meaning behind Joseph's words "God meant it for good in order to *bring about* . . ."[2] The Hebrew word translated here as *bring about* is a construction term.[3] It describes a task or building project akin to the one I drive through every morning. The state of Texas is rebuilding a highway overpass near my house. Three lanes have been reduced to one, transforming a morning commute into a daily stew. The interstate project, like human history, has been in development since before time began. Cranes hover overhead daily. Workers hold signs and shovels, and several million of us grumble. Well, at least I do. *How long is this going to last?*

———

My next-door neighbors have a different attitude toward the project. The husband and wife are highway engineers, consultants to the department of transportation. They endure the same traffic jams and detours as the rest of us but do so with a better attitude. Why? They know how these projects develop. "It will take time," they respond to my grumbles, "but it will get finished. It's doable." They've seen the plans.

By giving us stories like Joseph's, God allows us to study his plans. Such disarray! Brothers dumping brother. Entitlements. Famines and family feuds scattered about like nails and cement bags on a vacant lot. Satan's logic was sinister and simple: destroy the family of Abraham and thereby destroy his seed,

———

Jesus Christ. All of hell, it seems, set its target on Jacob's boys.

But watch the Master Builder at work. He cleared debris, stabilized the structure, and bolted trusses until the chaos of Genesis 37:24 ("They . . . cast him into a pit") became the triumph of Genesis 50:20 ("life for many people").[4]

God as Master Weaver, Master Builder. He redeemed the story of Joseph. Can't he redeem your story as well?

———

CHAPTER 3

You'll Get Through This

You'll get through this. You fear you won't. We all do. We fear that the depression will never lift, the yelling will never stop, the pain will never leave. Here in the pits, surrounded by steep walls and angry brothers, we wonder, *Will this gray sky*

ever brighten? This load ever lighten?
We feel stuck, trapped, locked in.
Predestined for failure. Will we ever exit
this pit?

Yes! Deliverance is to the Bible what
jazz music is to Mardi Gras: bold, brassy,
and everywhere.

Out of the lions' den for Daniel, the
prison for Peter, the whale's belly for
Jonah, Goliath's shadow for David, the
storm for the disciples, disease for the
lepers, doubt for Thomas, the grave
for Lazarus, and the shackles for Paul.
God gets us through stuff. *Through* the
Red Sea onto dry ground (Ex. 14:22),
through the wilderness (Deut. 29:5),
through the valley of the shadow of
death (Ps. 23:4), and *through* the deep
sea (Ps. 77:19). *Through* is a favorite
word of God's:

———

When you pass *through* the
	waters, I will be with you;
And *through* the rivers, they shall
	not overflow you.
When you walk *through* the fire,
	you shall not be burned,
Nor shall the flame scorch you.
	(Isa. 43:2)[1]

It won't be painless. Have you wept your final tear or received your last round of chemotherapy? Not necessarily. Will your unhappy marriage become happy in a heartbeat? Not likely. Are you exempt from any trip to the cemetery? Does God guarantee the absence of struggle and the abundance of strength? Not in this life. But he does pledge to reweave your pain for a higher purpose.

It won't be quick. Joseph was

---

seventeen years old when his brothers abandoned him. He was at least thirty-seven when he saw them again. Another couple of years passed before he saw his father.[2] Sometimes God takes his time: One hundred twenty years to prepare Noah for the flood, eighty years to prepare Moses for his work. God called young David to be king but returned him to the sheep pasture. He called Paul to be an apostle and then isolated him in Arabia for perhaps three years. Jesus was on the earth for three decades before he built anything more than a kitchen table. How long will God take with you? He may take his time. His history is redeemed not in minutes but in lifetimes.

But God will use your mess for good. We see a perfect mess; God sees a perfect chance to train, test, and teach the

---

future prime minister. We see a prison; God sees a kiln. We see famine; God sees the relocation of his chosen lineage. We call it Egypt; God calls it protective custody, where the sons of Jacob can escape barbaric Canaan and multiply abundantly in peace. We see Satan's tricks and ploys. God sees Satan tripped and foiled.

Let me be clear. You are a version of Joseph in your generation. You represent a challenge to Satan's plan. You carry something of God within you, something noble and holy, something the world needs—wisdom, kindness, mercy, skill. If Satan can neutralize you, he can mute your influence.

The story of Joseph is in the Bible for this reason: to teach you to trust God to trump evil. What Satan intends for evil,

God, the Master Weaver and Master Builder, redeems for good.

Joseph would be the first to tell you that life in the pit stinks. Yet for all its rottenness doesn't the pit do this much? It forces you to look upward. Someone from *up there* must come *down here* and give you a hand. God did for Joseph. At the right time, in the right way, he will do the same for you.

————

CHAPTER 4

Keep Calm and Make a Plan

We can't always see what God is doing.

But can't we assume he is up to something good? Joseph faced a calamity of a global scale. It had been two years since the last drop of rain. No rain meant no farming. No farming meant no food.

Yet Joseph assumed God was in the crisis.

Then he faced the crisis with a plan. He collected grain during the good years and redistributed it in the bad. When the people ran out of food, he gave it to them in exchange for money, livestock, and property. After he stabilized the economy, he gave the people a lesson in money management. "Give one-fifth to Pharaoh, and use the rest for farming and eating" (Gen. 47:24, author's paraphrase).

The plan could fit on an index card. "Save for seven years. Distribute for seven years. Manage carefully." Could his response have been simpler?

Could it have been more boring?

Some flamboyance would have been nice. A little bit of the Red Sea opening, Jericho's walls tumbling, or was-dead

———

Lazarus walking. A dramatic crisis requires a dramatic response, right? Not always.

We equate spirituality with high drama: Paul raising the dead, Peter healing the sick. Yet for every Paul and Peter, there are a dozen Josephs. Men and women blessed with skills of administration. Steady hands through whom God saves people. Joseph never raised the dead, but he kept people from dying. He never healed the sick, but he kept sickness from spreading. He made a plan and stuck with it. And because he did, the nation survived. He triumphed with a calm, methodical plan.

In the days leading up to the war with Germany, the British government commissioned a series of posters. The idea was to capture encouraging slogans on paper and distribute them about the country. Capital letters in a distinct typeface were used, and a simple two-color format was selected. The only graphic was the crown of King George VI.

The first poster was distributed in September of 1939:

YOUR COURAGE
YOUR CHEERFULNESS
YOUR RESOLUTION
WILL BRING
US VICTORY

Soon thereafter a second poster was produced:

FREEDOM IS
IN PERIL
DEFEND IT
WITH ALL
YOUR MIGHT

———

These two posters appeared up and down the British countryside. On railroad platforms and in pubs, stores, and restaurants. They were everywhere. A third poster was created yet never distributed. More than 2.5 million copies were printed yet never seen until nearly sixty years later when a bookstore owner in northeast England discovered one in a box of old books he had purchased at an auction. It read:

KEEP
CALM
AND
CARRY
ON

The poster bore the same crown and style of the first two posters. It was

———

never released to the public, however, but was held in reserve for an extreme crisis, such as invasion by Germany. The bookstore owner framed it and hung it on the wall. It became so popular that the bookstore began producing identical images of the original design on coffee mugs, postcards, and posters. Everyone, it seems, appreciated the reminder from another generation to keep calm and carry on.[1]

Of all the Bible heroes, Joseph is the one most likely to have hung a copy on his office wall. He indwelt the world of ledgers, flowcharts, end-of-the-year reports, tabulations, and calculations. Day after day. Month after month. Year after year. He kept a cool head and carried on.

You can do the same. You can't

———

control the weather. You aren't in charge of the economy. You can't undo the tsunami or unwreck the car, but you can map out a strategy. Remember, God is in this crisis. Ask him to give you an index card–sized plan, two or three steps you can take today.

Seek counsel from someone who has faced a similar challenge. Ask friends to pray. Look for resources. Reach out to a support group. Most importantly, make a plan.

Management guru Jim Collins has some good words here. He and Morten T. Hansen studied leadership in turbulent times. They looked at more than twenty thousand companies, sifting through data in search of an answer to this question: Why in uncertain times do some companies thrive while others

---

do not? They concluded, "[Successful leaders] are not more creative. They're not more visionary. They're not more charismatic. They're not more ambitious. They're not more blessed by luck. They're not more risk-seeking. They're not more heroic. And they're not more prone to making big, bold moves." Then what sets them apart? "They all led their teams with a surprising method of self-control in an out-of-control world."[2]

In the end it's not the flashy and flamboyant who survive. It is those with steady hands and sober minds. People like Roald Amundsen. In 1911 he headed up the Norwegian team in a race to the South Pole. Robert Scott directed a team from England. The two expeditions faced identical challenges and terrain. They endured the same freezing temperatures and unforgiving environment. They had equal access to the technology and equipment of their day. Yet Amundsen and his team reached the South Pole thirty-four days ahead of Scott. What made the difference?

Planning. Amundsen was a tireless strategist. He had a clear strategy of traveling fifteen to twenty miles a day. Good weather? Fifteen to twenty miles. Bad weather? Fifteen to twenty miles. No more. No less. Always fifteen to twenty miles.

Scott, by contrast, was irregular. He pushed his team to exhaustion in good weather and stopped in bad. The two men had two different philosophies and, consequently, two different outcomes. Amundsen won the race without losing a man. Scott lost not only the race but

———

also his life and the lives of all his team members.[3]

All for the lack of a good plan.

You'd prefer a miracle for your crisis? You'd rather see the bread multiplied or the stormy sea turned glassy calm in a finger snap? God may do this.

Then again, he may tell you, "I'm with you. I can use this for good. Now let's make a plan." Trust him to help you.

If you haven't yet trusted God, you can do that now. Trust in him to help you through all of life's trials. It's as easy as A-B-C.

Admit. Admit your wrongdoing. Admit that you are a sinner in need of a Savior.

Believe. Believe that Jesus is who he says he is. The Savior of the world. Believe he did what the Bible says he

---

did. He died for your sins and mine. He vacated the grave, and he reigns as Lord over the world.

Commit. Commit your life to his cause. Confess your belief privately and publicly. Find a church where you can be baptized, and grow in your faith.

There is no fine print. A second shoe is not going to drop. God's promise has no hidden language. Let grace happen, for heaven's sake. Of all the things you must earn in life, God's unending affection is not one of them. You have it. Stretch yourself out in the hammock of grace.

Would you let him save you? This is the most important decision you will ever make. Why don't you give your heart to him right now? Go to God in prayer and tell him, *I am a sinner in need of grace.*

———

I believe that Jesus died for me on the cross. I accept your offer of salvation.
It's a simple prayer with eternal results.

Your Response

I believe that Jesus Christ is the Son of the Living God. I want him to be the Lord of my life.

_____
Signed

_____
Date

_____

Scriptures for Your Turbulent Times

When You're Hurting

As one whom his mother comforts,
So I will comfort you;
And you shall be comforted in Jerusalem.

ISAIAH 66:13

―――――

O Zion,
You who bring good tidings,
Get up into the high mountain;
O Jerusalem,
You who bring good tidings,
Lift up your voice with strength,
Lift it up, be not afraid;
Say to the cities of Judah, "Behold your
    God!"
Behold, the Lord GOD shall come with a
    strong hand,
And His arm shall rule for Him;
Behold, His reward is with Him,
And His work before Him.
He will feed His flock like a shepherd;
He will gather the lambs with His arm,
And carry them in His bosom,
And gently lead those who are with
    young.

ISAIAH 40:9-11

Blessed are those who mourn,
For they shall be comforted.

MATTHEW 5:4

The Lord is near to those who have a
   broken heart,
And saves such as have a contrite spirit.

PSALM 34:18

For the Lamb who is in the midst of the
throne will shepherd them and lead them
to living fountains of waters. And God
will wipe away every tear from their
eyes.

REVELATION 7:17

When You're Grieving

Blessed are those who mourn, for they shall be comforted.

MATTHEW 5:4

Blessed be the God and Father of our Lord Jesus Christ, the Father of mercies and God of all comfort, who comforts us in all our tribulation, that we may be able to comfort those who are in any trouble, with the comfort with which we ourselves are comforted by God. For as the sufferings of Christ abound in us, so our consolation also abounds through Christ. Now if we are afflicted, it is for your consolation and salvation, which is effective for enduring the same sufferings which we also suffer. Or if we

are comforted, it is for your consolation
and salvation. And our hope for you is
steadfast, because we know that as you
are partakers of the sufferings, so also
you will partake of the consolation.
For we do not want you to be ignorant,
brethren, of our trouble which came
to us in Asia: that we were burdened
beyond measure, above strength, so that
we despaired even of life. Yes, we had the
sentence of death in ourselves, that we
should not trust in ourselves but in God
who raises the dead, who delivered us
from so great a death, and does deliver
us; in whom we trust that He will still
deliver us, you also helping together in
prayer for us, that thanks may be given
by many persons on our behalf for the
gift granted to us through many.

2 CORINTHIANS 1:3-11

———

And I heard a loud voice from heaven saying, "Behold, the tabernacle of God is with men, and He will dwell with them, and they shall be His people. God Himself will be with them and be their God."

REVELATION 21:3, 4

I will heal them and reveal to them the abundance of peace and truth.

JEREMIAH 33:6

When You Need Encouragement

And we know that all things work together for good to those who love God, to those who are the called according to His purpose.

ROMANS 8:28

The LORD has appeared of old to me,
    saying:
"Yes, I have loved you with an
    everlasting love;
Therefore with lovingkindness I have
    drawn you."

JEREMIAH 31:3

Now may our Lord Jesus Christ Himself, and our God and Father, who has loved us and given us everlasting consolation and good hope by grace, comfort your hearts and establish you in every good word and work.

2 THESSALONIANS 2:16, 17

When You Need Rest

For I have satiated the weary soul, and I have replenished every sorrowful soul.

JEREMIAH 31:25

"Remember the Sabbath day, to keep it holy. Six days you shall labor and do all your work, but the seventh day is the Sabbath of the LORD your God. In it you shall do no work: you, nor your son, nor your daughter, nor your male servant, nor your female servant, nor your cattle, nor your stranger who is within your gates. For in six days the LORD made the heavens and the earth, the sea, and all that is in them, and rested the seventh day. Therefore the LORD blessed the Sabbath day and hallowed it.

EXODUS 20:8-11

"Come to Me, all you who labor and are heavy laden, and I will give you rest. Take My yoke upon you and learn from Me, for I am gentle and lowly in heart, and you will find rest for your souls. For My yoke is easy and My burden is light."

MATTHEW 11:28-30

There remains therefore a rest for the people of God. For he who has entered His rest has himself also ceased from his works as God did from His. Let us therefore be diligent to enter that rest, lest anyone fall according to the same example of disobedience.

HEBREWS 4:9-11

Notes

Chapter 1: An Audacious Promise

1. Emphasis mine.

Chapter 2: Eventual Good

1. Spiros Zodhiates, ed., *The Hebrew-Greek Key Word Study Bible: Key Insights into God's Word, New American Standard Bible*, rev. ed. (Chattanooga, TN: AMG, 2008), Genesis 50:20. See also "Greek/ Hebrew Definitions," Bible Tools, Strong's #2803, *chashab*, www.bibletools.org/ index.cfm/fuseaction/Lexicon.show/ID/ H2803/chashab.htm.

2. The same term is used in Genesis 13:4 ("he had . . . *built* an altar" [NIV]), Job 9:9 ("He *made* the Bear"), and Proverbs 8:26 ("he *made* the earth" [NIV]).

3. Zodhiates, *The Hebrew-Greek Key Word Study Bible*, Genesis 50:20. See also *Strong's Exhaustive Bible Concordance Online*, #6213, www.biblestudytools.com/lexicons/hebrew/nas/asah.html.

4. Genesis 50:20 is from *The Message*.

Chapter 3: You'll Get Through This

1. Emphasis mine.

2. Joseph was probably seventeen when he was sold to the Midianites (Gen. 37:2). He was twenty-eight when the butler, who promised to help him get out of prison, was released (40:21–23). Two years later, when Joseph was thirty, Joseph interpreted Pharaoh's dreams (41:1, 46). And Joseph was about thirty-nine when his brothers came to Egypt the second time (45:1–6), in the second year of the famine following the seven years of plenty.

Tools for Your Church
or Small Group

You'll Get Through This
DVD
978-0-8499-5997-4 | $26.99

Max Lucado leads six video
sessions, which will help small
group participants apply the truth
of Genesis 50:20 to their own lives.
What Satan intends for evil, God
redeems for good.

You'll Get Through
This Study Guide
978-0-8499-5998-1 | $10.99

Filled with Scripture study,
discussion questions, and
practical ideas designed to
lead group members through
the story of Joseph and remind
us all to trust God to trump
evil, this guide is an integral
part of the *You'll Get Through
This* small group study.

Share the Promise

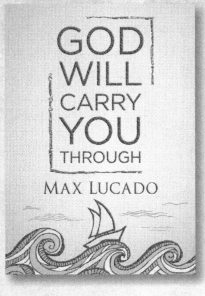

Personal stories of inspiration and faith

This beautifully designed, color, gift book offers
encouragement and renewed hope to anyone going
through a difficult time. Max invites readers to let
God's message guide them through tough situations.
Testimonies by everyday people, quotes, and Scripture
passages for meditation are woven throughout.

978-1-4003-2311-1 | $15.99

Chapter 4: Keep Calm and Make a Plan

1. "The Story of Keep Calm and Carry On," YouTube video, 3:01, posted by Temujin Doran, www.youtube.com/watch?v=FrHkKXFRbCI&sns=fb. See also *Keep Calm and Carry On: Good Advice for Hard Times* (Kansas City, MO: Andrews McMeel, 2009), introduction.
2. Jim Collins, "How to Manage Through Chaos," CNN Money, September 30, 2011, http://management.fortune.cnn.com/2011/09/30/jim-collins-great-by-choice-exclusive-excerpt.
3. Ibid.